P9-DNY-698

Tropical Fish

by Grace Hansen

ABDO
OCEAN LIFE
Kids

abdopublishing.com

Published by Abdo Kids, a division of ABDO, PO Box 398166, Minneapolis, Minnesota 55439.

Copyright © 2015 by Abdo Consulting Group, Inc. International copyrights reserved in all countries. No part of this book may be reproduced in any form without written permission from the publisher.

Printed in the United States of America, North Mankato, Minnesota.

102014

012015

THIS BOOK CONTAINS
RECYCLED MATERIALS

Photo Credits: Corbis, iStock, Shutterstock, Thinkstock

Production Contributors: Teddy Borth, Jennie Forsberg, Grace Hansen

Design Contributors: Laura Rask, Dorothy Toth

Library of Congress Control Number: 2014943650

Cataloging-in-Publication Data

Hansen, Grace.

Tropical fish / Grace Hansen.

p. cm. -- (Ocean life)

ISBN 978-1-62970-712-9 (lib. bdg.)

Includes index.

1. Tropical fish--Juvenile literature.   I. Title.

597--dc23

2014943650

Table of Contents

Tropical Fish

Tropical fish live in warm waters. They usually live near **coasts**.

Many tropical fish live
in coral reefs. Coral reefs
have lots of food. There
are many places to hide.

Clown Fish

Clown fish are tropical fish. Clown fish live in **sea anemones**.

9

Sea anemones protect clown fish. They sting other fish.

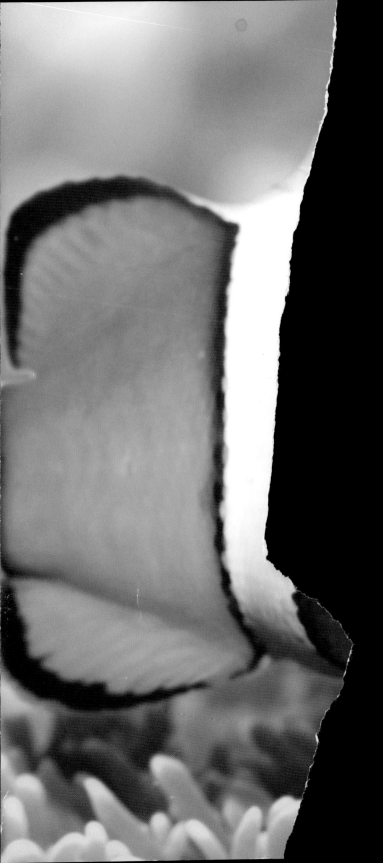

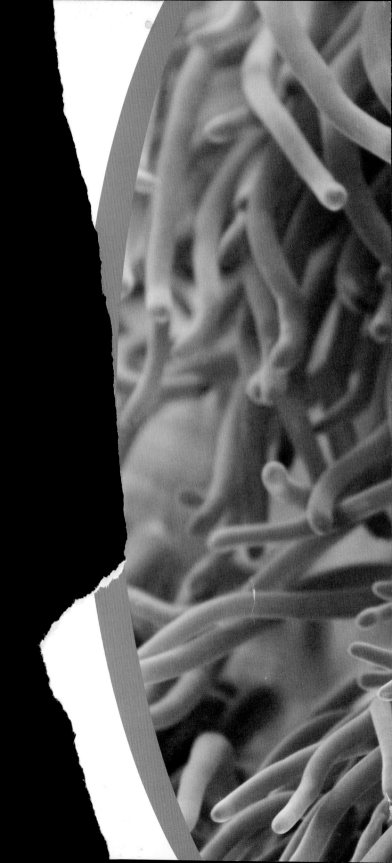

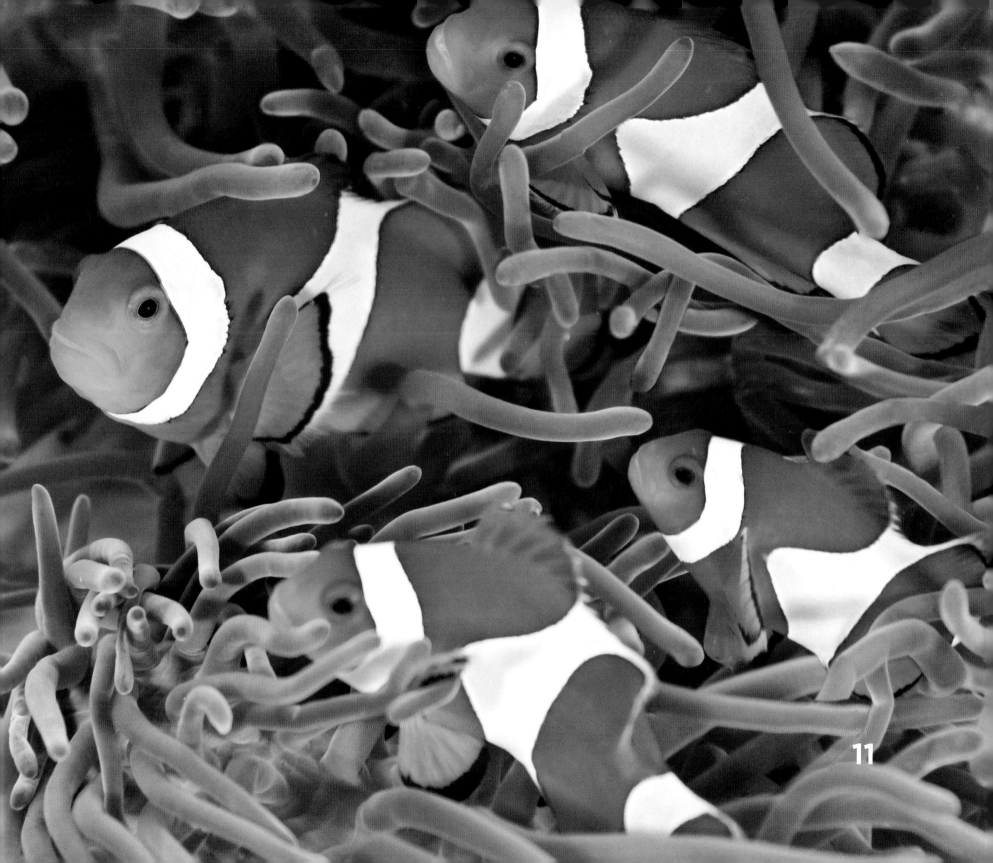

Angelfish

Angelfish are tropical fish.

They are bright in color.

They come in many **patterns**.

12

Angelfish are almost fearless.

They will swim with divers.

Tang Fish

Tang fish are tropical fish.

They are peaceful and gentle.

They are bright in color.

Lionfish

Lionfish are tropical
fish. They have stripes.
They have long spines.

19

The spines are **venomous**.

The venom can be deadly.

21

More Facts

- Clown fish do not just come in orange, black, and white. There are about 28 species of clown fish. They come in many different colors.

- Beautiful, peaceful tang fish live for a very long time. This makes them popular pets.

- Lionfish spread the fins on their sides to trap fish. This makes it easier to catch and eat their food.

Glossary

coast – land near an ocean.

pattern – a regular marking. Patterns may include stripes or spots.

protect – to keep safe.

sea anemone – a small, colorful animal that looks like a flower.

venomous – containing venom. Venom is poisonous.

Index

abdokids.com

Use this code to log on to abdokids.com and access crafts, games, videos, and more!

Abdo Kids Code:
OTK7129